An Instant Idea Book

January • February March

Instant Ideas for Elementary Teachers

by
Barbara Gruber & Sue Gruber

Illustrations by
Lynn Conklin Power

FS-8313 January-February-March

Copyright © 1988 Frank Schaffer Publications, Inc.
All rights reserved—Printed in the U.S.A.
Published by **Frank Schaffer Publications, Inc.**
1028 Via Mirabel
Palos Verdes Estates, California 90274

Table of Contents for January • February

Table of Contents for March

Introduction

January • February • March—Instant Ideas for Elementary Teachers provides a variety of bright ideas for winter months in your classroom. Activities are quick and easy to implement and fun for students.

Note! We have written three more Instant Idea books for you filled with exciting monthly activities. These books will help brighten every day in your classroom—all year long!

FS-8311 *September • October*
FS-8312 *November • December*
FS-8314 *April • May • June*

Barbara Gruber   *Sue Gruber*

January Ideas

Welcome January!

Have students make colorful posters for the month showing the January flower (carnation) and gemstone (garnet).

FS-8313 January-February-March

January Bulletin Board

Welcome the New Year with festive balloons!

Ideas for Captions:

- Welcome 19__!
- It's a Brand New Year!
- A Fresh Start
- New Beginnings

Directions:

1. Cover the bulletin board with paper of any color. Add a caption.

2. Have each student trace the balloon template on page 8 on two pieces of light-colored construction paper. Staple paper balloons together at the top and paste lined paper inside for writing.

3. Students decorate the front of the balloons. Have each person write a goal or resolution for the new year inside the balloon. Display the balloons on the bulletin board. Add a strand of yarn to each balloon.

4. For a festive touch, add paper streamers, musical notes and confetti!

Balloon Pattern

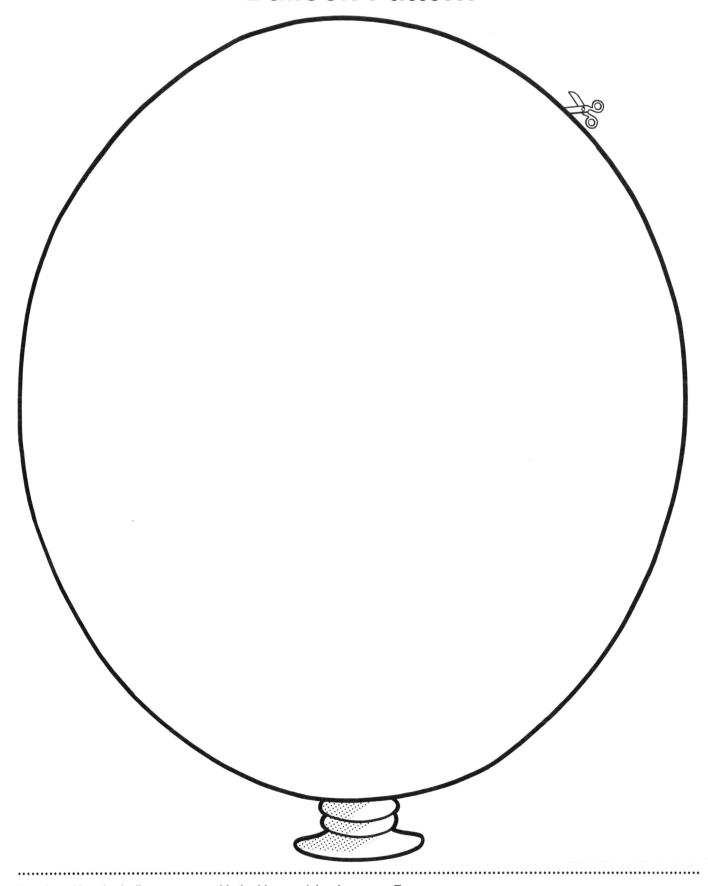

Teacher: Use the balloon pattern with the idea explained on page 7.

© Frank Schaffer Publications, Inc.

8

a reproducible page

FS-8313 January-February-March

January Vocabulary Activities

Instant Vocabulary Book

Take a few minutes to make an Instant Vocabulary Book to use all year long! Fasten ten 9" x 12" pieces of tagboard with binder rings as shown. Label each page with a month of the school year. Jot monthly vocabulary words on each page. As you think of additional words, add them to the appropriate pages. Keep this handy book on the chalk ledge for yourself and your students.

Idea! Number the words so you can do instant lessons like having children write the words from 10 to 16 in ABC order. See pages 10, 29, 30, 49, and 50 for additional vocabulary activities.

January

1. snow
2. white
3. cold
4. ice
5. birthday
6. King
7. history
8. peace
9. march
10. rights
11. new
12. year
13. melt
14. calendar
15. icicle
16. coat
17. hat
18. scarf
19. mittens
20. boots
21. shovel
22. skate
23. parka
24. ski
25. slip
26. slide
27. sled

Can You Remember?

Write the list of vocabulary words on the chalkboard. Have students look at the words for one minute. Then, cover the words and have students write as many as they can remember.

FS-8313 January-February-March

January Vocabulary Activities

Mystery Sentences

Students choose five words from the January vocabulary list. Next, they write a sentence for each word, leaving a blank space where the word should go. Then, students exchange papers and write in the missing words.

Amy Brown

1. There is _____ on the window.

2.

Pictionary

Have students choose 10 words from the list to write and illustrate.

Brian Ohara

mittens

snowflake

scarf

shovel

calendar

Categories

Have students sort the vocabulary words into groups of one-syllable, two-syllable and three-syllable words.

One Syllable
- new
- skate
- ski

Two Syllables
- birthday
- parka

Three Syllables
- history

FS-8313 January-February-March

January Writing Activities

The W I N T E R Writing Booklet

The Winter Writing Booklet can be used at any time during January, February or March. Reproduce page 12 for each student. Have students color and cut out the letters. Give each student a seven-page construction paper booklet. (Pages can be any size, but 6" x 9" paper works well.) Students paste the title on the cover and a letter on each page as shown.

Writing activity ideas for each letter:

Winter makes me think about...
    List 10 things.

Imagine a perfect day. Write about what would happen on the best day you can imagine.

Now is the time for winter sports. Make a list of five outdoor winter activities. Write the one you like best at the top of the list. Illustrate each activity.

Think about how you spend your time. Write down your daily schedule on school days and weekends. Add up the hours you spend on different activities like sleeping, eating, doing school work and watching television.

Embarrassing moments happen to everyone. Write about an embarrassing experience you have had.

Recess is a fun time at school. Pretend you are planning a playground for a school. Draw a picture of the playground equipment.

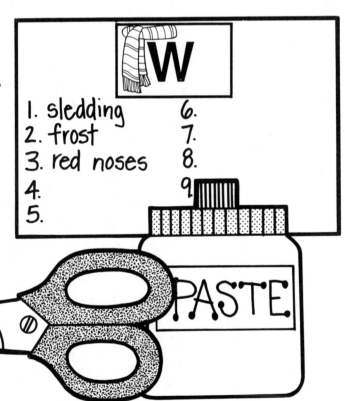

Helpful Hint! Work on the Winter Writing Booklet over a period of time. Collect and store the booklets after each assignment so they don't get lost!

 FS-8313 January-February-March

Winter Writing Booklet

Teacher: Use this page with "The Winter Writing Booklet" explained on page 11.

FS-8313 January-February-March

January Poetry Activities

Winter Poems

Write winter poems on a cold, wintry day! Tell students they are to write a four-line poem with the second and fourth lines rhyming.

Jot rhyming words on the chalkboard to make it easier for students to write their poems. For primary students, elicit ideas and write a poem together on the chalkboard.

Rhyming words:
snow, blow, glow
freeze, breeze, sneeze
bright, sight, night, light
cheery, dreary
sunny, funny
rain, main, pain, train

Cinquain Poems

Cinquain (sing KĀN) is a five-line form of unrhymed poetry that follows the pattern below. To help students understand how to write cinquain poems, write a poem on the chalkboard using ideas elicited from your students.

Line 1 One word (usually the title)
Line 2 Two words (describing line one)
Line 3 Three words (describing action)
Line 4 Four words (a feeling)
Line 5 One word (synonym for line 1)

FS-8313 January-February-March

January Science Activities

Benjamin Franklin, one of the founding fathers of our country, was a famous author, inventor, and scientist. He was born on January 17, 1706. Celebrate the birth of this famous American with these science activities.

Benjamin Franklin's Armonica

Franklin was intrigued by the musical sounds that were produced when a wet finger was rubbed around the rim of a water glass. He invented an instrument that used water and spinning glasses to make music. He called the instrument the armonica. You can make an instrument using glasses and water.

1. Line up eight drinking glasses or bottles that are all the same size. (Use glass, not plastic.)

2. Pour about one-half inch of water in the first glass. Continue filling glasses so each glass has more water than the previous glass as shown.

3. Tap each glass gently with a pencil or spoon. Listen to the different tones that are produced. Try to play a song on the musical glasses.

Absorb and Reflect Heat With Color

Franklin conducted experiments on heat absorption by different colors. He learned that dark colors absorb more heat than light colors. Try this activity to determine which colors absorb heat and which reflect it.

1. Cover one milk carton with black construction paper and one with white.

2. Fill each carton with ice cubes and place them in the sunlight.

3. Wait one hour. Check to see which carton has less ice.

4. The carton with less ice absorbed more heat. Which color absorbs more heat, white or black?

January Holidays and Special Days

My Time Capsule

Give each student a small box (boxes that bank checks come in are perfect) or a plastic egg from pantyhose to make a time capsule. Students put a variety of items in the time capsule. Students may include:

- a photograph of themselves
- the name of a favorite song
- the name of a favorite TV show
- a sample of their best handwriting
- a drawing of a future career
- the title of a book they have just read

Have students seal and label the time capsules as shown. Collect and store the capsules until the last day of school. Then, let students open them.

Talking Toys

Tell students to pretend to be one of their favorite toys. Have them write (or dictate to you) a short story in which they are the toy.

Have students draw their toys, cut them out and display them on a bulletin board with the stories. For a cute bulletin board, pin long strips of black construction paper in horizontal rows to resemble toy shelves. Then pin the paper toys on the shelves. Post the stories about the toys around the shelves.

15

January Holidays and Special Days

Weather Watchers

Keep track of the weather in January on a weather chart! Color a square on the graph to record each day's weather. At the end of the month, have a class discussion to interpret the weather graph. This graph is also a good source for math activities. For example, say... "There were eleven sunny days and fourteen cloudy days. Find the difference. What fraction of the days in January were rainy?"

Winter Rebus Stories

Reproduce page 17 for each student. Tell students to color and cut the pictures apart and use them to write sentences or a Winter Rebus Story. Blank squares are provided for students to draw pictures of their own. What fun for intermediate grade students to write rebus stories for younger students!

Winter Rebus Story

Draw pictures in the blank boxes.
Color the pictures and cut them apart.
Write a story using pictures in place of words.

Teacher: Use this page with "Winter Rebus Stories" explained on page 16.

17

a reproducible page

FS-8313 January-February-March

January Holidays and Special Days

A Famous Seamstress

Betsy Ross was born on January 1, 1752. She was a seamstress in Philadelphia, Pennsylvania. Many people think she made the first American flag with stars and stripes.

Have each student design a flag. Students plan their flags on 12" x 18" paper. Then, they make a flag using colored construction paper. Display the flags for all to see!

Ideas for flags:

school flag
classroom flag
family flag
all-about-me flag
city flag
theme flag
   (dinosaurs, flowers)

A Clever Code Maker

Louis Braille, born on January 4, 1809, was blinded in an accident at age three. While attending a school for the blind as a teenager, he invented the Braille alphabet for the blind. Louis adapted a code used by soldiers for sending messages at night. Braille is a system of raised dots which form 63 different characters.

Reproduce page 19 for each student. Have students use a pencil to write their first name in dots using the Braille code. To let students know what Braille feels like, have students turn their papers over, hold them up to the light, and poke a pin through each dot. Have students turn their papers back over and try to "read" their names by lightly sliding their finger tips over the raised part of the dots.

The Braille Alphabet

A B C D E F G H I
J K L M N O P Q R
S T U V W X Y Z

The Braille Alphabet

A	B	C	D	E	F	G	H	I
J	K	L	M	N	O	P	Q	R
S	T	U	V	W	X	Y	Z	

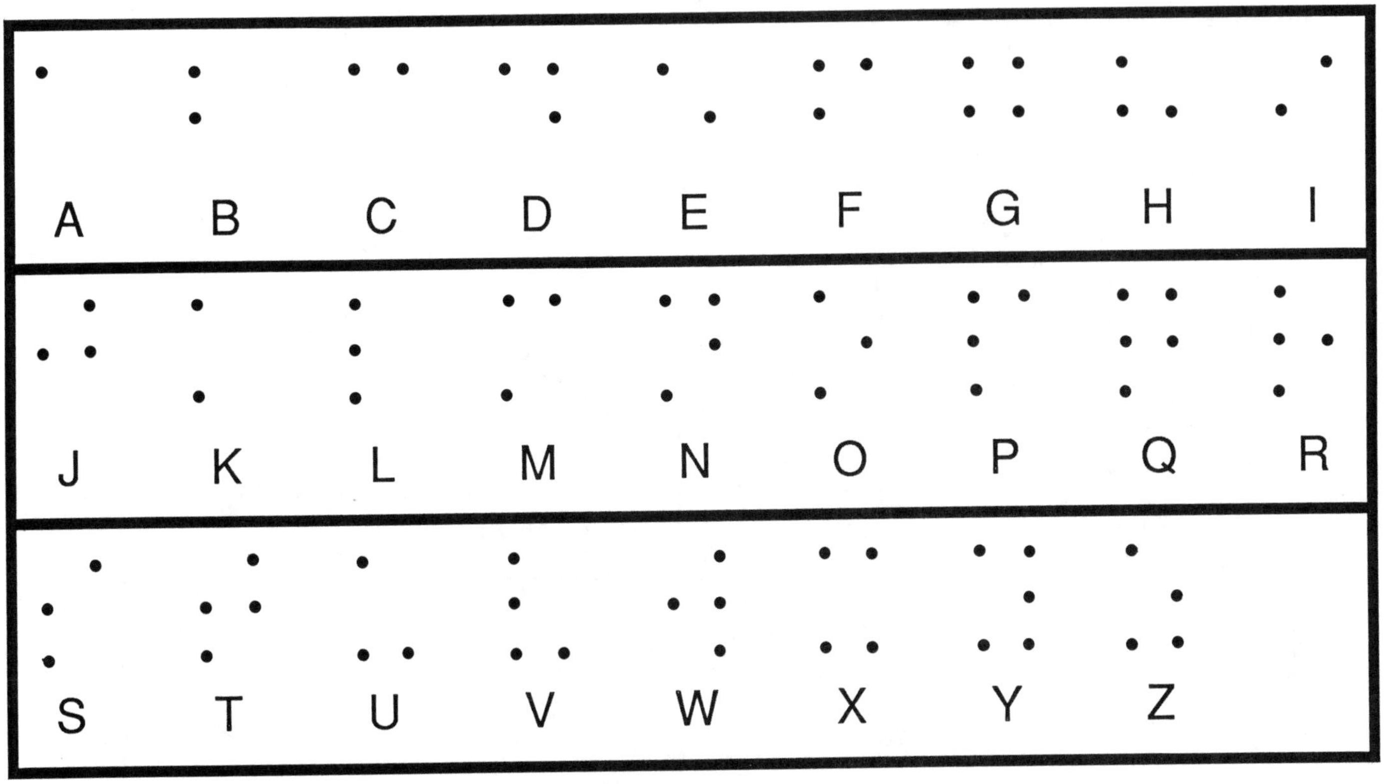

My name is _____

A message in Braille:

_____

_____

_____

Teacher: Use this page with "A Clever Code Maker" explained on page 18.

FS-8313 January-February-March

January Holidays and Special Days

Happy Birthday, Jakob Grimm! Jakob Grimm was born January 4, 1785. He and his brother Wilhelm, born February 24, 1786, wrote down familiar folk and fairy tales. Celebrate the world of fairy tales during the month of January with these high-interest activities.

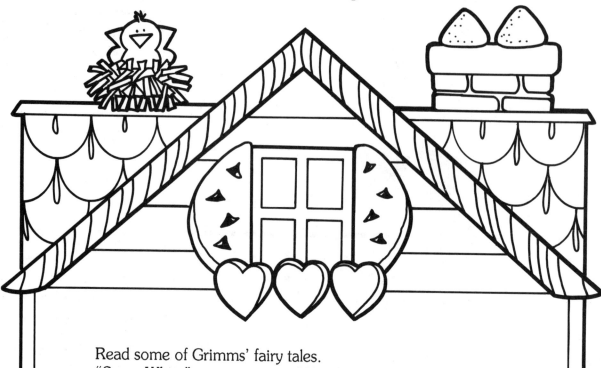

Read some of Grimms' fairy tales.

"Snow White"	"The Elves and The Shoemaker"
"Hansel and Gretel"	"The Frog-King"
"Rumpelstiltskin"	"The Fisherman and His Wife"
"Sleeping Beauty"	"Cinderella"

Make a fairy tale bookmark.
Design a book jacket.
Write a different ending.
Draw and label your favorite characters.
Write a summary.
Make a roll movie.
Write about your favorite parts.
Draw a series of three pictures to illustrate an exciting event.
Make a shoebox diorama.
Make a clay model of a character.
Write your own fairy tale.
Make a poster.

FS-8313 January-February-March

January Holidays and Special Days

Benjamin Franklin was born in Boston, Massachusetts, on January 17, 1706. He was a scientist, inventor, writer, and American statesman. He is also known for his many sayings.

Wise Words From Benjamin Franklin

Discuss some of Franklin's sayings with your class. Many of them are about saving time and money. Have each student select a favorite saying and copy and illustrate it.

A penny saved is a penny earned.

Early to bed, early to rise,
Makes a man healthy, wealthy and wise.

When you are good to others, you are best to yourself.

Lost time is never found again.

Don't throw stones at your neighbors', if your own windows are glass.

See page 14 for two science activities based on Franklin's ideas.

A-Penny-Saved-Is-a-Penny-Earned Bank

Have students make a savings bank from a milk carton.

1. Open a small empty milk carton. Then rinse and dry it.

2. Staple or tape the top of the carton leaving an opening in the center for inserting coins.

3. Cover the carton with red or blue construction paper.

4. Add patriotic decorations as shown.

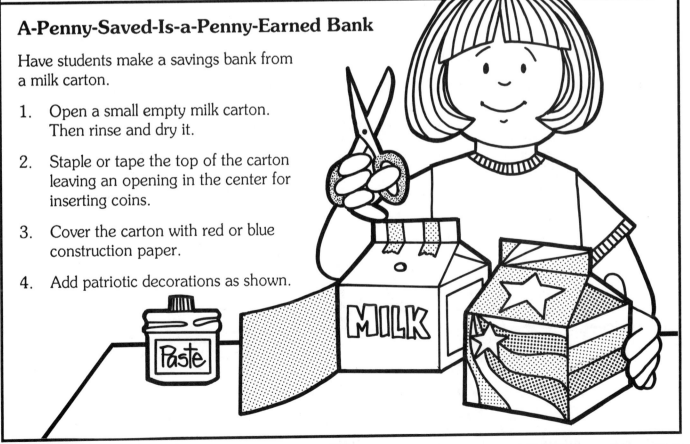

January Holidays and Special Days

World's Cleanest Desks!

The third Monday of January is National Clean Off Your Desk Day! What a perfect day for students and teachers to clean their desks! After desks are neat and clean, have students design a bumper sticker in honor of the day. Tape the bumper stickers to students' desks.

National Handwriting Day!

John Hancock, born on January 23, 1737, was the first to sign the Declaration of Independence. He signed his name in bold, beautiful handwriting. National Handwriting Day is celebrated on January 23, the anniversary of Hancock's birth.

Have students use construction paper scraps to design a handwriting award for themselves. At the end of the day or week, have each student select the best sample of his handwriting and attach the award to it.

January Holidays and Special Days

January Enrichment Activities

Use this activities list in a variety of ways. Select an activity for a class assignment or list the activities on the chalkboard as extra credit work.

Activities for students:

1. January is National Hobby Month. Draw a picture about your hobby. Ask your teacher if you can tell the class about it.

2. Alaska became the 49th state in January of 1959. Look up information about Alaska. Draw a poster showing the state bird, flower and flag for our 49th state.

3. January 4 is Trivia Day. Find an unusual fact about an animal. Tell it to two friends.

4. Make a list of different kinds of sports equipment used in winter (skis, ski poles, sleds, ice skates, hockey puck...). List the words in ABC order and illustrate each one.

5. January 16 is National Nothing Day. There are no holidays or celebrations on this date. Create a holiday for January 16. Make a poster about your holiday.

6. January 18 is the birth date of A. A. Milne who wrote *Winnie-the-Pooh*. Make a Winnie-the-Pooh card.

More Ideas for January

See pages 62–64 for a reproducible open skills worksheet, a parent newsletter, and handy notes.

February Ideas

Welcome February!

Have students make colorful posters for the month showing the February flower (primrose) and gemstone (amethyst).

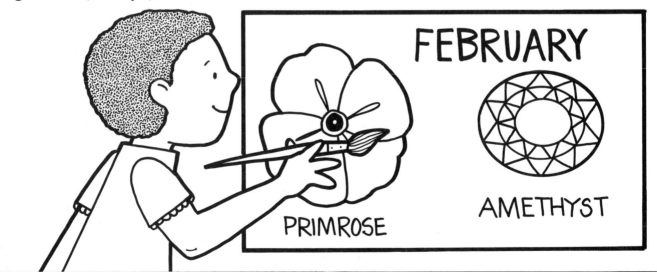

February Bulletin Board

February 1 is Freedom Day. Fill a bulletin board with liberty bells to celebrate the freedoms we enjoy in America.

Let Freedom Ring

Saul   Nancy   Jessica   Kevin

Ideas for Captions:

- Ring the Bell for Freedom
- Freedom Rings
- Freedom for All

Directions:

1. Cover the bulletin board with paper. Add a caption.

2. Use the bell pattern on page 28. Have students cut out the pattern, then trace and cut out another bell on light-colored paper. Students staple the bells together at the top and paste lined paper inside. Tell students to draw a crack on the left front of the bell.

3. Choose one of these phrases or activities for students to complete inside their bell.

I am proud to be an American because …
I have the freedom to…
Here is a poem about freedom.
Here is a list of words that describe what *freedom* means to me.

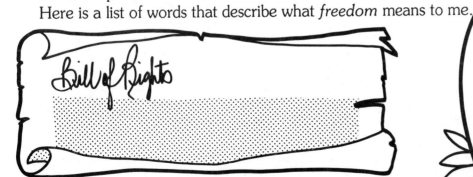

Liberty Bell Pattern

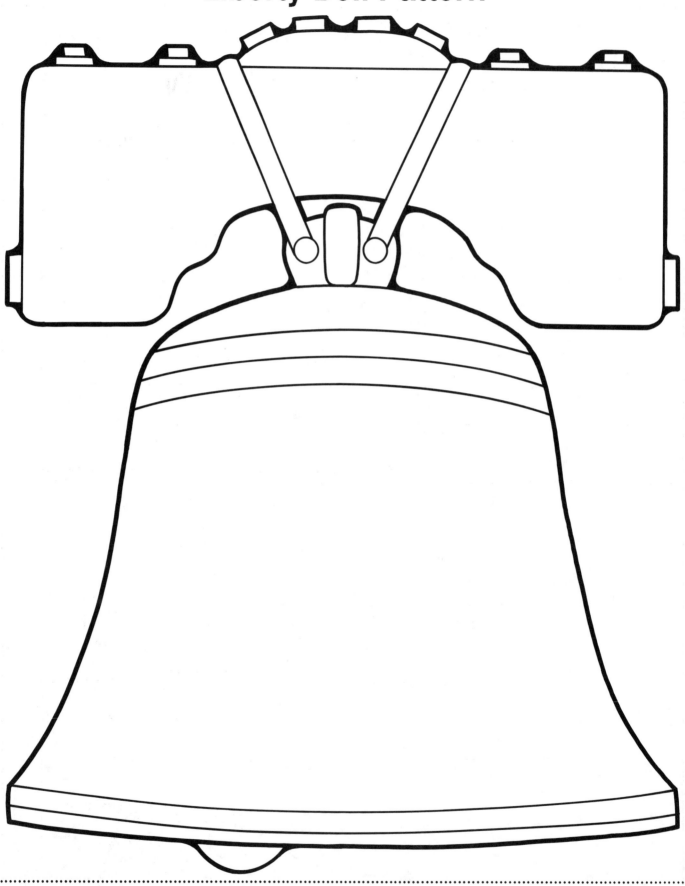

Teacher: Use the bell pattern with the February bulletin board explained on page 27.

FS-8313 January-February-March

a reproducible page

February Vocabulary Activities

Instant Vocabulary Book

Add these February words to your Instant Vocabulary Book (see page 9).

See the vocabulary activities on pages 9, 10, 30, 49 and 50.

February

1. red
2. white
3. pink
4. lace
5. card
6. valentine
7. groundhog
8. fourteenth
9. heart
10. cupid
11. president
12. holiday
13. Lincoln
14. Washington
15. mail
16. cherries
17. love
18. paper
19. friend
20. mailbox
21. honest
22. letter
23. party

Silly Sentences

Have students write silly sentences for vocabulary words. Each word in the sentence should start with the same letter. Tell students to use the dictionary to find words that start with the letter they are using.

Word: *cupid*

Sentence: Cute cupids carry cuddly creatures.

We want a white winter.

FS-8313 January-February-March

February Vocabulary Activities

The Love Bug

Cut out dozens of red or pink hearts. Give each student 8–10 hearts. Have students write a vocabulary word on each. Then, students make a love bug by pasting the hearts in ABC order and adding legs, antennae and a heart-shaped face.

Sentence Cut-Aparts

In large letters, have each student print a sentence that includes two vocabulary words. Tell students to be sure to start the sentence with a capital letter and end it with a punctuation mark. Now, students cut their sentences apart word by word. They scramble the words and exchange sentence cut-aparts with a partner. Students unscramble the sentence, paste it on art paper and illustrate it.

My Best Handwriting

Have students write each vocabulary word two times in their best handwriting. Then, tell students to underline in red crayon the best handwriting sample in each pair.

February Poetry Activities

February is International Friendship Month. Have students write a poem about a special friend.

Friends Forever

Have students write "A friend is..." on their papers. They write a friend's first name vertically on the paper. Tell students to go over the letters of the name with a red crayon and draw a heart around each letter. Using each letter, students write a quality of the person they especially like.

"February Days"

Your class will enjoy rehearsing and presenting "February Days"— a choral reading poem for February. Reproduce this poem found on page 32.

For kindergarten or first grade students, print the poem on the chalkboard and read it aloud together, or divide the class into seven groups and assign parts.

February Days

ALL: February has many special days,
That we can celebrate in lots of ways.

GROUP #1: It's winter and it's time for snow,
Listen to the cold winds blow.
Our heavy coats feel warm and nice,
Careful now! Don't slip on ice!

GROUP #2: Mr. Groundhog peeks from his hole,
Predicting springtime is his role.
If there is no shadow, then springtime is near,
If there is a shadow, winter stays we fear.

GROUP #3: Thomas Edison's ideas were bright,
We thank him for the electric light.
Science was important to this man,
For many inventions he had a plan.

GROUP #4: February 12—that's the date,
Lincoln's birthday—he was great.
Abe was honest, all could see,
He helped the slaves to be free.

GROUP #5: Valentine's Day is almost here,
Send a card to someone dear.
Valentine parties filled with fun,
A happy time for everyone.

GROUP #6: Washington's birthday—the 22nd day,
As our first president he led the way.
He and his soldiers crossed the Delaware River,
Bitter cold weather really made them shiver.

ALL: February has many special days,
That we can celebrate in lots of ways.

Teacher: Use this choral reading poem with "February Days" explained on page 31.

February Science Activities

Galileo Galilei, an Italian scientist, was born on February 15, 1564. At age 20 he made the first scientific observations that led to his law of the pendulum. Commemorate the birth of this famous scientist with this activity.

Time That Swings!

Find out if changes in the weight of a pendulum bob or the length of its string affect the rate at which a pendulum swings.

1. Make a pendulum by attaching a weight (washer, nut, fishing weight) to a thirty-inch piece of string.

2. Pull the weight back at about a 90-degree angle as shown and release.

3. Have students count how many times the pendulum swings back and forth in one minute. Record the number on the chalkboard.

4. Now shorten the string of the pendulum to fifteen inches and repeat steps 2 and 3 above. Record the results on the chalkboard.

5. Add an additional weight to the pendulum and repeat the experiment.

Length	Weight	Number of Swings	
30"	1 washer		
30"	2		
15"	1		
15"	2		

Try several different weights and lengths of string. Hold a class discussion about the results recorded on the chalkboard.

33

February Holidays and Special Days

February is International Friendship Month. Promote friendship in your classroom with these activities.

Meet My Friend

Group your students in pairs. Students interview their partners to find out their favorite food, television show, and weekend activity. Encourage students to spend at least one recess with their partner to get to know him or her better.

Set aside 10 minutes of each school day for the "Meet My Friend" presentation. Have one student begin by introducing her partner to the class in this way:

"I am happy to have you meet a friend of mine.

He likes… (share information gained in the interview).

May I present… (announce name of student)."

Then the student being presented comes to the front of the room and everyone applauds.

Give all students an opportunity to do a "Meet My Friend" presentation.

Howdy Partner!

Create a friendly, cooperative atmosphere in your classroom. Put students' names in an envelope. Draw two names at a time until you have paired up the whole class. Have partners work together on an activity such as:

- play a partner game
- read a story together
- work together on a picture
- test each other with flashcards
- work together on a class project

February Holidays and Special Days

Focus on friendship this month by doing something special for another class at school. As a gesture of friendship, students can make bookmarks and teach a fun-to-play game to another class.

Love Bug Bookmarks

Students use paper scraps to make bookmarks out of hearts. They then present the bookmarks to another class!

Four Corners Game

Make four construction paper signs numbered from one to four. Tape a number on the wall in each corner of your classroom. Make sure students understand that each corner has a number.

To play the game have one student be the "caller" and put his head down. Then say "Four Corners." Students may stand in any of the four corners. Then call out "Stop." The caller then calls out "one," "two," "three" or "four" to indicate which group of students must return to their seats. (If he calls out "four," students in that corner must sit down.) The game continues by saying "Four Corners" again. Students move around to a different corner. Eventually only one student will be left. By the process of elimination, one student will win the game. That student becomes the caller for the next round.

This game may also be played outdoors on the basketball court.

February Holidays and Special Days

In February we observe Black History Month and the birthdays of two famous presidents—Abraham Lincoln and George Washington. Plan a celebration with your students to honor these famous Americans.

A Day of Celebration

Decide on famous people you wish to honor. Jot a list of at least five people on the chalkboard. Choose a date on which to hold the celebration. Now, start to plan the festivities and include some of the following activities. Divide the class into groups to work on them.

Decorations and Invitations Group

Students create banners and signs announcing the upcoming celebration and design an official invitation.

Music and Books Group

Students select a song to sing or record to play at the celebration. They select an assortment of books about those being honored to display on a "Book Table."

Dramatic Reading Group

Each student reads aloud a selection about one of the honorees or the group presents the "February Days" choral reading poem on page 32.

Get-the-Facts Group

Students make a poster, banner or time line about each person being honored. The Decorations Group posts these around the classroom.

Have all students design an award from paper scraps for one of the honorees. If possible, show a film that ties in with the celebration on the day of the party.

February Holidays and Special Days

People Post Cards

Give each student a 5" x 8" index card or a piece of tagboard to make a people post card. Have students draw a famous person on the blank side of the card. On the other side, students address the card, draw a stamp, and write a message about the famous person.

Commemorative Coins

Cut circles two to three inches in diameter out of gray and gold paper. Students design unique coins to commemorate famous Americans.

FS-8313 January-February-March

February Holidays and Special Days

V I P Banners

Brighten your classroom with banners about very important people! Give each student an 18" x 24" piece of red, white, or blue butcher paper. Cut the bottom edge of the banner as shown. Have students paste pictures of and sentences about the VIP on the banner.

Attach the banner to a wire hanger by folding over the corners and stapling.

Stand-Up Time Line

Time lines are a perfect way for students to focus on milestones in the life of a famous person.

Each student cuts a 12" x 18" piece of construction paper in half lengthwise. He fan folds each half, then pastes the halves together by overlapping two edges. This forms a stand-up time line with eight sections.

February Holidays and Special Days

February is American Heart Month. Teach your class some indoor exercises to build up their cardiovascular system.

Take a Fitness Break!

Teach your students the sit-in-your-seat exercises below and on page 40. They are a terrific change of pace for your classroom. After taking a fitness break, students will find it easier to work quietly. Do the exercises to music. Have students clap their hands between exercises so everyone can start the next routine together.

Fitness Break Exercises
(Students sit at desks while exercising.)

Exercise #1

Raise, then lower your right shoulder.
Raise, then lower your left shoulder.
Raise, then lower your right shoulder.
Raise, then lower your left shoulder.
Raise, then lower both shoulders two times.

Exercise #2

Clap, then raise your right hand.
Clap, then raise your left hand.
Clap, then raise your right hand.
Clap, then raise your left hand.
Clap, then raise both hands.
Clap and raise both hands again.

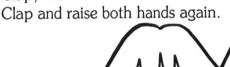

Exercise #3

Clap four times.
Tap your left shoulder with your right hand
  two times.
Tap your right shoulder with your left hand
  two times.

Exercise #4

Clap four times.
Tap your left elbow with your right hand
  two times.
Tap your right elbow with your left hand
  two times.

February Holidays and Special Days

Use these four classroom exercises to continue the fitness routine explained on page 39.

Exercise #5

Clap four times.
Tap your left knee with your right hand two times.
Tap your right knee with your left hand two times.

Exercise #6

Knock on your desk with both hands four times.
Clap four times.
Touch your left shoulder with your right hand four times.
Touch your right shoulder with your left hand four times.
Clap four times.

Exercise #7

Clap four times.
Shake your hands four times.
Clap four times.
Shake your hands four times.

Exercise #8

Place your hands on your hips.
Twist to the left four times.
Twist to the right four times.

February Holidays and Special Days

National Inventor's Day is celebrated during the first week of February. Get your students thinking of some great new ideas and inventions with these activities.

World's Greatest Invention

Tell your students to think of an invention that would help them get up and get ready for school. It might be a bed-making machine or a machine that selects their clothes. Students draw a color illustration of their invention, give it a name, and write about it.

Meet Thomas Alva Edison—An Amazing Inventor

Thomas Alva Edison patented one thousand ninety-three inventions. He was born on February 11, 1847. Have students present a play about this amazing inventor. Use the reproducible play on page 42.

Meet Amazing Thomas Edison

Cast: Announcer
  Reporter #1   Reporter #4
  Reporter #2   Thomas Edison
  Reporter #3   Father of Boy

ANNOUNCER:	Thomas Edison was born on February 11, 1847. During his life he patented over one thousand inventions.
REPORTER #1:	Thomas Edison was curious about almost everything. At age three, he sat on some goose and hen eggs and tried to hatch them.
REPORTER #2:	When Edison was in elementary school, children were not allowed to ask questions. Edison got in trouble for asking questions at school, so his mother decided to teach him at home.
REPORTER #3:	Thomas Edison wanted to do chemistry experiments at home. He got a job as a newspaper and candy salesperson to earn money for the chemicals needed in his experiments.
REPORTER #4:	One day, Thomas rescued a child from the railroad tracks. The child's father said:
FATHER OF BOY:	Thank you, young man. How can I repay you for saving my son's life?
THOMAS EDISON:	You are the telegrapher in the train station. Can you teach me to be a telegrapher?
REPORTER #1:	Thomas Edison worked as a telegrapher for several years. On the night of April 14, 1865 he received a message over the telegraph. It said:
REPORTER #2:	President Lincoln has been shot.
REPORTER #3:	Thomas Edison became a full-time inventor. His inventions, like the electric light and the phonograph, changed the way people lived.
REPORTER #4:	Thomas Edison said he had two secrets to success. His mottoes were:
THOMAS EDISON:	There is no substitute for hard work.
REPORTER #4:	And...
THOMAS EDISON:	Genius is one percent inspiration and ninety-nine percent perspiration.
ANNOUNCER:	I told you Thomas Edison was an amazing inventor. We hope you enjoyed our play.

....

Teacher: Use this play with the idea explained on page 41.

February Holidays and Special Days

Laura Ingalls Wilder was born on February 7, 1867 and died in 1957. She wrote books about her pioneer family. Her book *Little House on the Prairie* is a favorite of young readers.

The World of Laura Ingalls Wilder

Introduce your class to the "Little House" series of books. Read your class *Little House in the Big Woods,* the first book in the series. Then, show students the other books in the series and tell them which are available in the school library.

My Family Album

Students fold a piece of 12" x 18" construction paper in half to make a family album.

On the cover, they draw a family portrait. They paste lined paper inside and write about a family adventure. Then students illustrate the story.

February Holidays and Special Days

V I P Valentines

Your students will enjoy making valentines for very important people around the school. Paste or staple together two construction paper hearts to make an envelope for the cards. When students have extra time, they can work on a valentine. On Valentine's Day, have students deliver the cards to the VIPs.

Card Cut-Ups

Here is a clever way for students to make valentines. Have them follow these directions:

1. Fold 9" x 12" white art paper in half, then unfold.
2. Fold 9" x 12" red art paper in half and cut a heart as shown.
3. On the red paper, fold the left edge in and cut some small hearts and diamonds. Repeat this step with the right edge. Then unfold the cut out edges.
4. Paste the red paper on the white paper, pasting only the edge sections.
5. Decorate the front of the card with heart cutouts and your own design.
6. Write a message on the card.

February Holidays and Special Days

February Enrichment Activities

Use this activities list in a variety of ways. Select an activity for a class assignment or list the activities on the chalkboard as extra credit work for students.

Activities for students:

1. February is National Children's Dental Health Month. Make a poster about how to take good care of your teeth.

2. February is American Music Month. Draw a picture of yourself enjoying your favorite kind of music. Write a sentence about your picture.

3. Groundhog Day is February 2. Legend says that if the groundhog comes out of his hole and does not see his shadow, spring will come early. If he does see his shadow, there will be another six weeks of winter weather. Draw a cartoon strip about the groundhog on February 2.

4. Make a list of ways you can help each person in your family on Valentine's Day.

5. Write a poem about a special day in February. Your poem does not have to rhyme.

6. Presidents' Day is celebrated the third Monday in February. Make a poster showing the President of the United States, the White House, and the American flag.

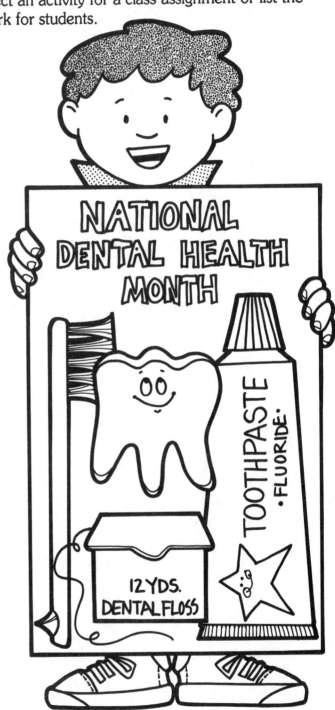

More Ideas for February

See pages 62–64 for a reproducible open skills worksheet, a parent newsletter, and handy notes.

March Ideas

Welcome March!

Have students make colorful posters for the month showing the March flower (violet) and gemstone (aquamarine).

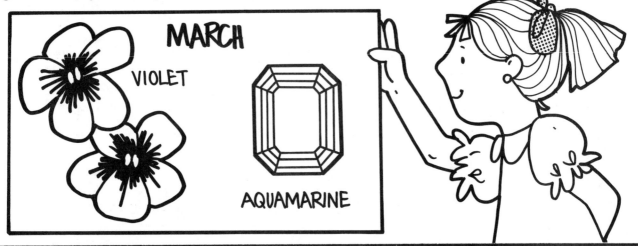

MARCH

VIOLET

AQUAMARINE

March Bulletin Board

Salute Francis Scott Key with a patriotic bulletin board. Key wrote the words to "The Star-Spangled Banner" during a battle in the War of 1812. On March 3, 1931, the song was adopted as the national anthem of the United States.

Oh! Say Can You See...

Pete Martin

ARIZONA

Debi Spur

I love America.
It's so nice.
I love the lakes.
Sue Walton

Ideas for Captions:

- America the Beautiful
- Proud and Patriotic
- Proud to Be an American
- We Salute Our Country

Directions:

1. Cover the bulletin board with paper in a bright patriotic color. Add a caption.

2. Have each student color and cut out a copy of the drum on page 48.

3. On the front of the drum, students do one of these activities:

   - Draw a picture of the American flag.
   - Write a poem about America.
   - Draw a picture of your state flag.

4. Add a few musical notes cut from black construction paper, as shown, to embellish the bulletin board.

Drum Pattern

FS-8313 January-February-March

a reproducible page

March Vocabulary Activities

Instant Vocabulary Book

Add the March words to your Instant Vocabulary Book (see page 9). Use the vocabulary activities on pages 9, 10, 29, 30, and 50.

March

1. lion
2. lamb
3. windy
4. Kite
5. shamrock
6. lucky
7. green
8. Irish
9. holiday
10. history
11. women
12. clouds
13. raindrop
14. shower
15. robin
16. puddle
17. St. Patrick
18. leprechaun
19. umbrella
20. weather
21. health
22. breezy
23. nest
24. gentle

What's Missing?

Have students choose 10 words from the vocabulary list. Students write the words leaving out the consonants. Then, they exchange papers with a partner and fill in the missing letters.

_io_
_e
_o_i_

Shamrock Scrabble

Have students work with a partner. Give each pair of students a copy of Shamrock Scrabble on page 50. Have students cut the 36 letter tiles apart and place them face down on the desk. Each student takes 18 letter tiles. Each tile with a large shamrock may be used to represent any letter. When you say "Go," each student makes as many words as she can with her tiles. At the end of three minutes, call out "Stop." Players add up the points for each word they made. Each letter is worth one point. They subtract the points for the letter tiles they did not use to get a total score. The student in each pair with the most points is the winner.

Idea! Tell students they can make words separately or in a crossword puzzle format. Remind them that names cannot be used for words.

Shamrock Scrabble

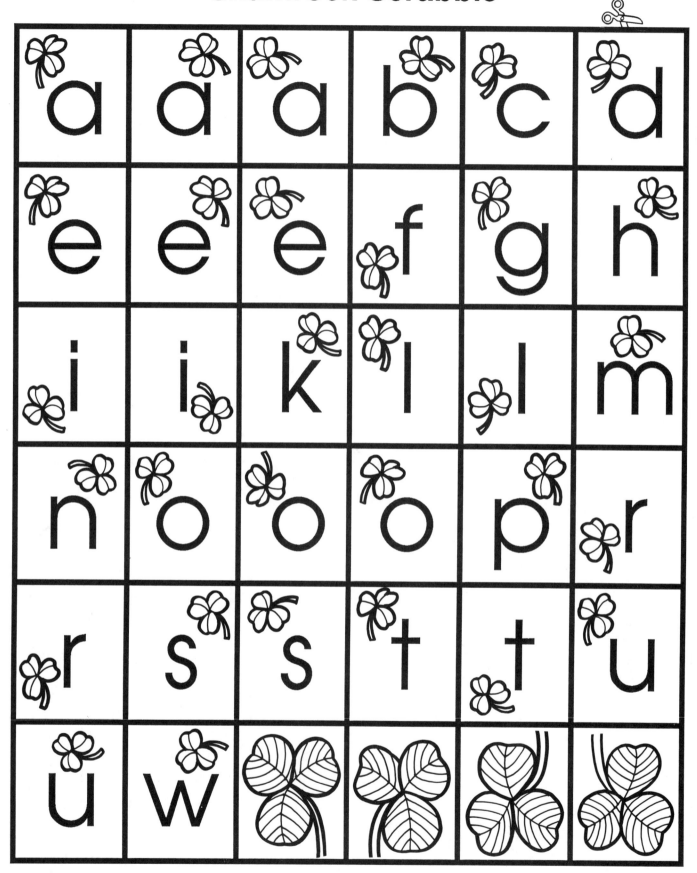

FS-8313 January-February-March

March Poetry

Pitter-Patter Poetry

Here's the perfect poetry writing activity to brighten a rainy day. Have students write a haiku poem about the rain. After they write a practice copy, have students write their poems inside a raindrop as shown.

Haiku Pattern

Line 1 has five syllables.
Line 2 has seven syllables.
Line 3 has five syllables.

Rain lightly falls down,
Covers the ground with raindrops,
Now flowers will grow.

How to make raindrops:

Make several tagboard patterns for raindrops. Have students trace a raindrop pattern two times on blue construction paper. Staple the two raindrops at the top as shown. Paste the haiku poem inside the raindrop. Use paper scraps to decorate the front of the raindrop with flowers, butterflies, trees and birds.

March Science Activities

Luther Burbank, a famous American horticulturist (plant breeder), was born on March 7, 1849. Burbank worked hard to improve plants and to develop new ones through hybridization. Honor this important scientist with these experiments!

Plants Have Roots!

Rooting vegetables in a glass or jar is a wonderful way for students to learn about the root systems of plants. Use toothpicks to suspend the vegetables in water as shown. Use sweet potatoes, turnips, yams, or avocado seeds. (Plant potatoes and turnips with the narrow end in water. Plant avocado seeds with the narrow end pointing up.)

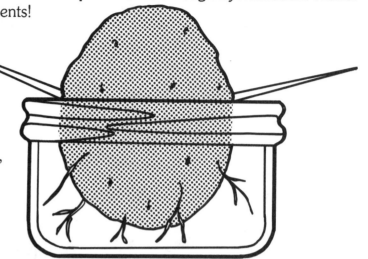

Plants Have Stems!

Demonstrate how water moves through stems to the leaves of plants with this activity. Place a stalk of celery in a glass of water with red or blue food coloring added. Have students observe what happens over a three-day period.

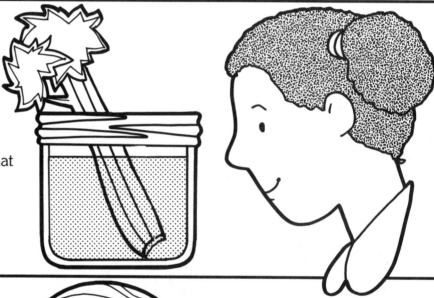

Plants Have Leaves!

Students will enjoy learning about the structure of plant leaves with this activity. Students arrange the leaves of several plants on their desktop. They place art paper over the leaves and rub with the flat edge of a crayon to make a rubbing. Students will observe veins in the leaves on the crayon rubbing.

FS-8313 January-February-March

March Holidays and Special Days

March is Youth Art Month! A classroom art gallery is a wonderful way to show off your students' artistic talent.

Our Art Show

Each student does one art project for the art show. You will want to display a variety of artwork done in different media. Think about the different kinds of art supplies available for students. Then, assign each student a particular medium.

Ideas:
crayon
chalk
charcoal
pencil
watercolor
oil paint
tempera paint

Give each student a 9" x 12" sheet of art paper. To make an interesting exhibit, group artwork by its medium (watercolors, crayon drawings...).
Invite another class and staff members to see the art show!

Idea! To display artwork, make a paper easel from strips of black construction paper as shown.

Lion and Lamb Banner

March weather often comes in roaring like a lion and goes out like a lamb gently, with a touch of spring. Have students make a Lion and Lamb Banner for the month of March.

1. Reproduce page 54 for each student. Have students color and cut out the patterns.

2. Each student glues his patterns onto a sheet of 12" x 18" green construction paper. Students can decorate the banners with paper scraps.

3. Fold three pieces of 2" x 8" orange construction paper in half. Glue them (folded side up) to the top of the banner.

4. To hang each banner, thread yarn through the folded pieces of orange paper.

Name _____

Lion and Lamb Banner

M	A
R	C
	H

Color and cut out.
Glue on your banner.
Decorate.

March Comes in Like a Lion
and Goes out Like a Lamb

March winds like a lion roar.
Rain clouds—it's going to pour.
Warmer days—it feels like spring.
Soon the birds will start to sing.

54

FS-8313 January-February-March

Teacher: Use these banner patterns with the "Lion and Lamb Banner" explained on page 53.

March Holidays and Special Days

National Nutrition Month is celebrated in March. Focus on healthful eating in your classroom with these activities.

The Lunch Swap

Assign each student a partner. Give each student a piece of art paper. Students draw and color the foods they would pack in a nourishing lunch for their partner. Students cut out the "foods" and put them in a brown lunch bag.

Let's Eat Right!

Students use the reproducible worksheet on page 56 to keep track of the foods they eat in a day. At the beginning of a school day, tell students to record the foods they ate for breakfast. Do this again after lunch. Also have students write down any snacks they have eaten that day. Collect the papers. Tell students that the next morning they will be asked to fill in the foods they had for dinner and additional snacks.

After the Let's Eat Right worksheet has been completed, discuss food groups with your class. Then, have students use a yellow crayon to circle all breads and cereals on their worksheets, a green crayon to circle fruits and vegetables, a red crayon for meats, and a blue crayon for dairy foods. Have students count how many foods they've eaten from each group. Have them list foods they should eat more of and foods they should eat less of.

Let's Eat Right

Write down the foods you eat in one day.

Breakfast

Lunch

Dinner

Snacks

Teacher: Use this page with "Let's Eat Right" explained on page 55.

56
a reproducible page

FS-8313 January-February-March

A Great Moment in History

Cast: Announcer #1
Announcer #2
Alexander Graham Bell
Thomas A. Watson
Announcer #3
Announcer #4

ANNOUNCER #1: Alexander Graham Bell was born in Scotland on March 3, 1847. When he grew up, he became a teacher of deaf children.

ANNOUNCER #2: Bell was interested in experimenting with electricity. He had an idea for a machine that would make it possible for people to talk over long distances. He and his assistant, Thomas A. Watson, experimented for years.

BELL: Oh, Watson, why doesn't it work? We can hear sounds but not words over the wire.

WATSON: We're making progress, Alexander. Be patient.

ANNOUNCER #3: Then, it finally happened...one day, in the laboratory...

[Alexander and Watson are in different rooms.]

BELL: Well, now I want to try this new transmitter. Oh no, I spilled acid on my clothes. MR. WATSON, COME HERE. I WANT YOU!

WATSON: By golly, Alexander, we've DONE it.

[He runs to Bell, waving his arms wildly.]

BELL: What are you talking about? Help me get this acid off my clothes.

WATSON: Alexander, I heard you over the wire. Success at last!

ANNOUNCER #4: Bell and Watson traveled around the country demonstrating how the telephone worked.

···

Teacher: Inventor Alexander Graham Bell was born on March 3, 1847. On March 10, 1876 he sent the first telephone message. Recreate this important moment in history with this reproducible play.

March Holidays and Special Days

Wildlife Week is in March. The goal of wildlife conservation is to protect and preserve our wild plants and animals.

Info-Marks!

Info-marks are better than bookmarks! They are used as bookmarks but they have important information on them for students to read! Have your students make a set of info-marks to use in your classroom. Why not make an extra set for another class or for the school library?

Cut tagboard or construction paper into 3" x 12" strips, one strip for each student in the class. Write the name of a wild plant or animal on each strip. Give each student a strip. Have students illustrate the plant or animal in full color and add information on the info-mark!

Idea!

Other topics for info-marks:

- famous people
- famous places
- prehistoric animals
- the United States
- events in American history

Bumper Stickers

Give each student a 6" x 18" strip of construction paper. Students create bumper stickers about protecting wildlife. Display the bumper stickers on a bulletin board!

March Holidays and Special Days

Many people wear green on March 17 to celebrate St. Patrick's Day. Join in the spirit of the day with these activities!

Shamrock Spelling Practice

Cut dozens of shamrocks from green construction paper. Have students write each spelling word on a shamrock. Then, have students paste the shamrocks on paper in ABC order.

For sentence writing, have students paste the shamrock shapes on their papers instead of writing the words.

Shamrock Plant Stick

Tape a plastic drinking straw between two construction paper shamrocks to make a plant stick. Pop it in a plant to add a special touch!

Find the Shamrock

Students will enjoy this classroom game!

1. One player is "It" and leaves the room.

2. The other students are seated. Give one student a shamrock cut from green paper. This student hides the shamrock by sitting on it.

3. The student who is It returns to the room and tries to find out who is sitting on the shamrock. To gather clues about where the shamrock is hidden, he stands in five different areas of the classroom. In each area, students clap loudly if he is near the shamrock and softly if he is far from where it is hidden. After standing in five places, he has three chances to guess who is sitting on the shamrock.

4. If he guesses correctly, he becomes It again. If he doesn't guess correctly, the person sitting on the shamrock becomes It.

March Holidays and Special Days

Fun Mail Week starts the second Sunday in March. Have your class fill an envelope full of fun-to-get goodies for another class in your school. Include:

- a funny picture drawn by a student
- some riddles copied from riddle books
- cartoons clipped from the newspaper
- a letter or story
- some stickers

Have a student deliver the fun mail to the lucky class!

National Goof-Off Day

On March 22 it's perfectly okay to goof off a bit.

- Tell students their homework assignment is to goof off.

- Have a ten-minute goof-off period. Put a sign on the door saying: DO NOT DISTURB!

- Have each student list and illustrate 15 things he likes to do when goofing off.

 FS-8313 January-February-March

March Holidays and Special Days

March Enrichment Activities

Use this activities list in a variety of ways. Select an activity for a class assignment or list the activities on the chalkboard as extra credit work .

Activities for students:

An apple a day keeps the doctor away.

1. March is National Peanut Month. George Washington Carver, who lived from 1864 to 1943, made over three hundred products from the peanut. Draw a picture showing what you like best about peanuts. Write a sentence about your picture.

2. March 7 is the birthday of horticulturist Luther Burbank. Burbank, who lived from 1849 to 1926, developed many new kinds of fruits, flowers, vegetables and trees. Make a colorful poster showing your favorite fruit, flower, vegetable and tree. Label each picture.

3. International Women's Day is March 8. Write a note to a woman you admire. Tell her why you think she is special.

4. Johnny Appleseed Day is March 11. Johnny Appleseed, whose real name was John Chapman, lived from 1774 to 1847. He planted many apple orchards. Use your best handwriting to write this saying about apples: *An apple a day keeps the doctor away.*

5. Make a card to give to someone on St. Patrick's Day. Put a badge made from green paper inside the card.

6. March winds are perfect for flying kites. Cut a kite shape from construction paper. Add a yarn tail and some paper ties. Use crayons to decorate the kite.

More Ideas for January, February and March

Add directions and a skill activity to the reproducible open worksheet on page 62. Use skills such as math facts, synonyms, antonyms, syllables, or rhyming words.

Use "In the News" on page 63 to write a newsletter for parents. Reproduce a copy for each child to take home.

Reproduce page 64 to use for quick notes to parents, students, and colleagues! They can also be used as award certificates!

Name _____ Skill: _____

Pick a Pair!

Directions: _____
_____

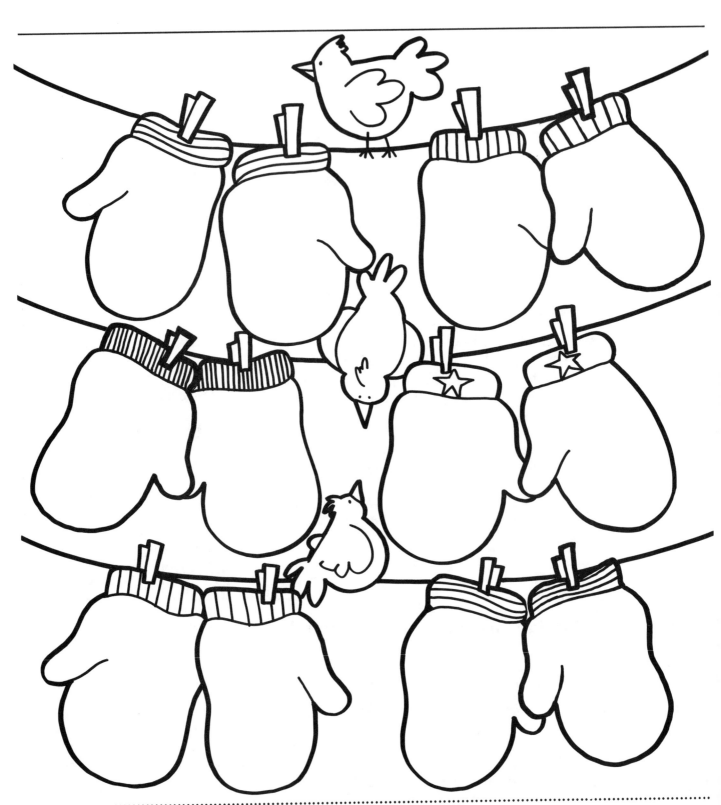

FS-8313 January-February-March

In the News

To _____ From _____ Date _____

_____

_____

_____

_____

_____

_____

_____

_____

_____

_____

_____

_____

_____

_____

Teacher: Directions for using this newsletter are on page 61.

63
a reproducible page

FS-8313 January-February-March

From

To

From

To

From

Teacher: Use these decorated notes for quick messages to parents, students, and yourself.

© Frank Schaffer Publications, Inc.

64

a reproducible page

FS-8313 January-February-March